ALWAYS SOMETHING ELSE:
URBAN ASIA AND AFRICA AS EXPERIMENT

AbdouMaliq Simone

ALWAYS SOMETHING ELSE:
URBAN ASIA AND AFRICA
AS EXPERIMENT

Basler Afrika Bibliographien

Basler Afrika Bibliographien
Namibia Resource Centre & Southern Africa Library
Klosterberg 23
P O Box 2037
CH 4051 Basel
Switzerland
www.baslerafrika.ch

CARL SCHLETTWEIN
STIFTUNG

The Basler Afrika Bibliographien is part of the Carl Schlettwein Foundation

Cover photograph: Street scene in Kankan, Guinea
(picture: Till Förster, 2012)
Editors: Rita Kesselring, Caro van Leeuwen, Pascal Schmid
Layout and typesetting: Tilo Richter

ISBN 978-3-905758-81-8
ISSN 2297-7058

FOREWORD

African cities are a challenge in many ways. They challenge urban councils and planners who try to direct their development in a way that makes them inhabitable for the many that flock into the urban space from the hinterland. They challenge the daily skills of their inhabitants who must make ends meet. They challenge sedimented social practices and the mere sociability of those who live the city as their social space. They challenge conventional conceptions of what a built environment must provide to those who, later, appropriate it in unforeseen ways. The challenges are legend. Many generations will still have to face them.

Not least, the stunning growth of African cities — today the fastest worldwide — questions scholarly imaginations of the urban. Our knowledge of how cities grow and how they shape the lives of their inhabitants is largely based on the experience of our own, Western history. Georg Simmel's classical ideas about the overwhelming experience of urban sounds and sights seem to be a mere shadow of what African urbanites have to face day in and day out. Forcefully, African cities seem to refute Louis Wirth's association of city life with modernity in all its dimensions; the loss of local culture, the disintegration of family ties, the weakening bonds of kinship and solidarity, and more generally the undermining of 'tradition'. There is little left of urban studies that remains unquestioned by the mere existence of African cities and the multiple ways of urban life they breed: Kinship still underpins bonds of solidarity while simultaneously new forms of support and solidarity emerge. Urban life produces infinite forms of popular culture that can be as local as older forms while also embracing the latest global trends of hip-hop and rap music.

Since 2001, AbdouMaliq Simone, one of the strongest voices in the analysis of the conundrum that cities in the Global South pose, speaks of the worlding of African cities. Always in the making, these cities appropriate from all sides—be they local, national, regional or global — whatever their populace finds useful or attractive for whatever they as actors may aim at. The basis for this historically unprecedented flexibility is an extraordinarily high degree of segmentation—a feature of the social as well as economic and material dimension of the urban that links back to older, mainly anthropological studies of African societies. It is sometimes misunderstood as fragmentation that inhibits the growth and the emergence of more stable urban structures. Simone, however, sees it as one of the most important pillars that allow African urbanites to make a living despite all obstacles and to render their cities into inhabitable urban spaces— the subject of the Schlettwein Lecture that he delivered on 22 October 2014.

Because such cities show a sort of lightness in all forms of social life, they defy all attempts at regulating, at planning them in the same way a city in the Global

North would be organized. Urbanity manifests itself in forms that strike many different chords. While urban elites may fancy prestigious construction projects that display architecture of high modernism, the youth living only a few steps away from these sites but nonetheless at the margins of this cultural and social space may simultaneously articulate their disdain for the city as a showcase of modernisation and development ideologies. They may use all forms of street art to make themselves visible and assert their right to the city. Black graffiti walls may testify to their misery—walls with gloomy depictions of young men with hidden faces, holding microphones who sing about having no prospects for a better life since all ways to prosperity are blocked by older generations. Yet, these young men live an urban life, based on all sorts of income, including petty crime. Such articulations of aspirations are an essential part of urbanity—as much as four lane streets and the splendid architecture the urban elite would admire.

African cities disprove simple dichotomies. Neither local versus global nor urban versus rural will serve as analytical instruments. They merge into each other as the actors unfold their own agency. Spaces that older urban theory would call peri-urban are manifold geographies of transition. Local and global are referenced simultaneously in a bewildering wealth of social practices. Ways of life, which outsiders would qualify as thoroughly rural, co-exist and eventually merge with urban sociality. Urbanites make their cities in ways that scholars yet have to comprehend, notwithstanding the ground-breaking and highly seminal work of Simone and a few other urban scholars who look at African cities as sites where conventional urban theory is constantly contested.

For the incredible flexibility, that lightness of urban life where everybody may become somebody else and do something else overnight is also a burden. Many Africans living their cities would indeed prefer a more stable and more reliable infrastructure, would love to have more predictable perspectives for their future and that of their children. Yet they would not want to give up what urban life offers them today. They will make use of their creativity to develop their cities further. Cast into long-term research questions developed at the Centre for African Studies Basel, this is what the University of Basel seeks to address in the future with newly created positions in Urban Anthropology; History and Theory of Architecture and Urbanism; and Architecture, Urban and Territorial Design as well as one position in Urban Studies at the African Centre for Cities of the University of Cape Town. This focus on African cities and the rural-urban nexus extends and strengthens the African Studies network at the University of Basel as well as our cooperation with African partners.

Korhogo, 17 January 2016
Till Förster

URBAN LIFE WHERE IT CANNOT BE LIVED

Many African and Asian cities and urban regions are considered bastions of the uninhabitable. They are the homes of marginalized black and brown bodies that cannot really be homes because their environments are incompatible to what normally would be required for human sustenance. Because these cities are widely considered to be the "responsibility" of those who inhabit them, the fact that they appear as uninhabitable also renders their inhabitants not really or fully human.

There is a cruel irony in all of this, as some of the most "spectacular" of urban built environments, architectural and engineering feats are also taking place right next to apparent wastelands, further eroding long-honed, albeit problematic, sociability (Fu and Murray 2014, Marshall 2013, Roy and Ong 2011).

That large numbers of these inhabitants were, and continue to be extracted from Africa and Asia, so that a global economy could be conceived and materialized elsewhere—once through slavery, and now through both forced and voluntary migrations—constitutes an inextricable dependency of the fully human on those considered not. It also solidifies the conditions through which that dependency can be disavowed or produced as a relationship of fundamental, natural inequality. That many

African and Asian urban regions remain inundated with an underclass thus is proof of the normality of an uneven distribution of space that either will not be overcome or alternately, is rectified only through an almost unfathomable deployment of effort and resources (DiMuzio 2008, Ghertner 2010, Gidwani and Reddy 2011, Heron 2011). This view also suggests that a definitive and unyielding image of urban efficacy and human thriving exists and should be the object of aspiration by those living in supposedly uninhabitable spaces (Heller and Evans 2010, Legg 2007, Roy 2009, Shepherd et al. 2013).

Questions about what is inhabitable or not have long defined the nature and governance of urban life (Adams 2014, Foucault 2009, Thacker, 2009). There is also a massive, variegated literature that articulates the relationships among dispossession, the expropriation of resourcefulness, the constitution of property, the dissolution of collective solidarities, the circumscription of maneuverability, the imposition of law, and the autonomy of market, and in doing so, accounts for the figuration of what counts as urban habitation (Amin 1974, Bhalla and Lapeyre 1997, Blomley 2004, Chakrabarty 2000, Chaudhury 2012, Glassman 2011, Glassman and Samatar 1997, Hart 2002, Harvey 2003, King 1989, Lubeck and Walton 1979, McCann and Ward 2010, Peck et al. 2009, Rossi 2013, Sparke 2007).

Without denying the ravages of long-term structural impoverishment to which many African and Asian cities are subjected, what if the so-called uninhabitable does not necessarily point to a depleted form of urban life but simply a different form—one that constantly lives under specific threats and incompletion. But as long as our imaginations, policies and governing practices adhere to a tightly drawn sense of what constitutes normal humanity, it is difficult to recognize such urban life as a generative difference (Huyssen 2008, Robinson 2013). As long as cities or large swathes of territory within them are seen as fundamentally uninhabitable, as incapable of generating new capacities, and in dire need of rescue and remaking through the massive infusion of external resources or a renewed commitment to a vast repertoire of disciplinary tools, the critical impetus from which to make these cities something else than they are now is lost.

As Gilles Deleuze (1995) would indicate, these different modes of the habitable cannot be part of an overarching program of development for a particular social body or territory; they do not presume the existence of a living entity to which they contribute. Rather maneuvers toward such equity of possibilities must disrupt the calculations that assume a particular kind of distribution of authority or capacity among pre-existent identities. Instead, the focus might be on the emergent figurations of social bodies constituted through the intersections of different ways of inhabiting the urban. "It is because of the action of the field of individuation that such and such differential relations and such and such distinctive points (pre-individual fields) are actualized" (247). As Achille Mbembe (2013) indicates, inhabitants, situated in the cross-fires of multiple trajectories of sense and subjugation take and do what they can to create fugitive, slippery spaces, always under the grip of some imposed redemptive maneuvers, which never quite succeed.

Given the persistence of base subjugations operating under the auspices of a continuously inventive capitalism, which has promised to leave colonially imposed differences far behind (Chakrabarty 2012), how is it possible to upend the distinctions between the inhabitable and uninhabitable as clear demarcations of specific dispositions? How might they be seen as operations of subterfuge or critique—practices that take nothing for granted, that lend stability and possibilities of transformation to the precarious or undermine the pretensions of all which is considered secure? At the same time, we do need to retain these distinctions as a way of stopping ourselves from thinking that no matter what crises and conditions people face, that somehow resilient adaptation is always possible.

Based on long term work in urban Africa and more recently Jakarta, this essay attempts to generate some strategic reflections on how to think about such an interstice of effaced and sustained distinctions between the habitable and inhabitable. This is particularly done in the context of accelerated transformations and obduracies in mega-urban regions of what was considered to be the Global South. I want to explore some of the ways in which the habitable and uninhabitable are and can be *redescribed* in terms of each other.

The cities from which most of the ethnographic details are drawn here, though major metropolitan areas in their own right, have historically been at the fringes of where normative urban planning and policymaking has been constituted. While significant arguments have been made as to the salience of the urban margins for generating "pilot projects" in urban development later generalized to the metropoles of economic and political power (King 1989, Wright 2002), the persistent singularities of urban processes in cities like Kinshasa and Jakarta are not easily mobilized to disarm this normative. Nevertheless, they pose a swirling of details that continuously grate against, circumvent, or infect the materializing of particular instantiations of the urban, and which open up the possibilities of many rhythmic modulations of the relationships between power, policy, and popular practices. This is what Valentina Napolitano (2015) calls "the part of an urban re-articulation (that) has become the material trace of a knotting of histories and condensation of fears, violence, intimacies and forms of belonging" (57).

The cities invoked here are long subjected to imperial and colonial projects of varying traction, violence, and efficacy. Places like Kinshasa, Khartoum, and Jakarta were built with all kinds of complicities, seductions, and betrayals, and as such they exude ambiguous, troubling memories etched into the built environment. They, nevertheless, retained the *details* of what might have been, of projects only partially realized, of collectively self-constructed built environments that sometimes demonstrated inordinate capacities to create viable livelihoods out of dispersed fragments. But they also could reveal messy, unwieldy, and often violent natures that pushed and pulled people and materials in all kinds of directions, throwing them off balance and thus into a lifetime of half-baked compensations.

In the extension of urbanization across a planetary trajectory, these details are seemingly subject to an unprecedented effacement, even as variously scaled urban regimes mobilize them as materials to enable the emplacement of investment and speculation (Brenner and Schmid 2015). Kinshasa and Jakarta, different as they are from each other, as they are from everywhere else, may not be the epicenters from which critique of the urban normative might be most effectively issued. Still, the uncertain interfaces of their relationships with the larger world, reflected in both the speed at which they are being remade and the endurance of long-honed capacities to build economies through collaborative social relations, make them critical sites in this project of redescription—states of existence that *might* be.

In an era where the normality of any standardized version of humanity is continuously upended in the constantly mutating assemblages of biological, technological and digital materials, notions about what constitutes normal urban residence continue to be applied to the ways in which the value and efficacy of African and Asian urbanities are judged. A supposedly countervailing move, whereby the resilience and resourcefulness of those who have almost nothing is emphasized, ends up reiterating these same versions. This is because resilience is usually couched in a form of surprise, a kind of "yes, even the poor have a way of proving their humanity." Surviving the uninhabitable then becomes testament to a human will and capacity that minimizes the impact of injustices of past and present (Dawson 2009). It feeds into claims that if only the inhabitants of these cities would do what humans are truly capable of doing, and really apply their skills of survival to the urgencies at hand, then new cities would be truly possible (Amin 2013, MacKinnon and Derickson 2013).

Those that inhabit the supposedly uninhabitable are subject to seemingly endless lists of deprivation. Hundreds of research projects have demonstrated clear correlations between health, mortality, environmental conditions, economic poverty, spatial exclusion, racial identity, and political justice. But to what extend do these indices of deprivation and violence simply normalize as uninhabitable the places where many people attempt to make a life? Normative moral inclinations would seem to render intolerable conditions that shorten lives, waste potentials, and produce debilitating traumas, misery, and chronic illness. Such inclinations would seem to compel the alleviation of suffering and the empowerment of human capacity.

But we have to consider the extent to which these moral inclinations get in the way of seeing and understanding the collective memories, the exchanges and reciprocities, the breakthroughs and failures, and the material residues of countless efforts to endure through conditions that are perceived and experienced in many different ways by these residents. While survival entails what has to be done, endurance considers what "ought to be done" (Negarestani 2014). The two do not necessarily intersect or remain separate, and both are operative in the everyday lives of those who occupy the uninhabitable. There is the creation and relationship to a ground, a place, and an infrastructure of individual and collective existence, no matter how provisional, improvised, or run-down.

In cities where the machinery of decision-making, planning, resource allocation, and service provision hobbles along in bureaucratic ineptness, improvised deals, and massively skewed distributions, the majority of inhabitants still largely rule their worlds. They do so to the extent that they continuously construct and update the practices, designs, and materials that are put to work in engineering spaces of inhabitation. Perhaps more importantly, many continue to reticulate the experiences, skills, perceptions, and networks of the people around them in order to materialize circuits through which needed goods, services, and information pass (Bayat 2010, Benjamin 2008, Chattopadhyay 2006, McFarlane 2011a, Nielsen 2011).

EVERYWHERE AND NOWHERE
IS HABITABLE

In many respects the uninhabitable is an anachronistic concept. Not simply in the fact that people have long built homes and economic activities on the surfaces of the most ruined and dire conditions. But also in the ways in which the uninhabitable, or what Austin Zeiderman (2013) calls "living dangerously", is used as the medium through which certain segments of cities are able to compel recognition of their existence. Additionally, they secure services and opportunities that would be beyond their grasp if they did not pose themselves as a population at risk. Habiting the uninhabitable then becomes the means through which the poor may enter into various entanglements of provisioning and compliance, where they gain a foothold as normative citizens, and where the severity of the risks they face reiterate rather than challenge the functionality of liberal urban governance.

Additionally, as Sally Sargeson (2013) points out in her examination of the expropriation of rural land in China, urbanization acts through a violence that demeans rural existence and inflicts long-lasting harm. "Re-zoning land for urban construction and expropriating it thus become means of resolving the purported problems of collective ownership, of transforming rural land and housing from dead capital into fungible assets that can be sold, leased and mortgaged, and spurring cycles of building, refurbishment, demolition and rebuilding. The violence of property definition, exclusion, land use regulation, zoning and expropriation constitutes urban development" (1076).

The uninhabitable is a tricky concept given the global drives to render everything habitable no matter the quality. The impetus toward habitation appears across different scenarios and backgrounds. For example, while desert cities have existed for a long time, the massive conversion of desert climates into urban regions demonstrates a kind of perverse triumph of the built environment over physical terrain, albeit at enormous resource costs. This may be a long way from squatting on rubbish piles or covering squalid creeks with makeshift shanties. But it does point to a conviction that cities can refigure complex ecologies with complex adaptations and insulate themselves from adverse surroundings. That even the best-engineered cities succumb to volatile weather and floods is not yet a sufficient deterrent to this conviction.

That much of Asia acted as fodder for the proof of developmental dreams—the fact that backward economies, with determined and sometimes coercive governmental action and inward financial flows, could produce well-planned, thriving metropolises—and that Africa now seems posed to follow in these footsteps points to this sense of endlessly renewable habitation. But something else may also be going on, for some cities seem to expand without clear economic logic.

Take Kinshasa for example, the world's poorest city of its size. Although the historic core of the city fronts a semi-circled river which acts as a national boundary—limiting the trajectories of where the city's physical growth can take place—the real boundaries of the city expand exponentially each year so that one can still claim to be inside Kinshasa some 90 kilometers from that historic core. It is hard to precisely determine the demographics of the city. Depending on whom you talk to, its size ranges from 9 to 15 million, which is a lot of uncertainty, and even GIS analyses are hard pressed to come up with reasonably accurate figures. Allowing for even the vast tracks of land near the center that are tied up as military encampments or the remnants of colonially demarcated buffer zones, much of the city hovers across tightly packed nodes dispersed across long distances.

So while many opportunities for systematic infilling may exist, the near universal perception in Kinshasa is that the city is moving elsewhere. As a result, many inhabitants hurry to stake their claims at ever-shifting peripheries, which still seem to be in the middle of nowhere. In order to maintain a staked claim, a household has to implant someone on site in order to protect it, as the relative newness and vacancy of these areas mean that households stay where they are for the moment. As this sense of expansion is materialized in all directions away from the river, households are also concerned about missing the "real action", so they will also stake additional claims in completely different parts of the city's periphery. While the actual acquisition of new property may not consume large amounts of money, the fact that households have to support some kind of physical presence in these different locations, run back and forth between them along congested roads, and still maintain household economies in the place where they have been all along and have been barely making it as it is, results in substantial expenditures of time and money.

As large numbers of residents are swept up in this anticipation, their efforts indeed urbanize the periphery, with markets, schools, churches, and outposts of administrative offices. The rendering of the bush into extensions of Kinshasa is in part driven by the "old standard" of escalating land values through speculation and the infusion of external finance that jacks up property prices in older residential districts near the commercial core. Yet there is something almost evangelical in the determination of *Kinois* to stretch the city, as if these efforts offer some redemptive compensation for all of the difficulties most of them face just putting bread on the table.

As Filip de Boeck (2011, 2012) and with his colleague Marie-Françoise Plissart (2004), in his magisterial writings on the city points out, Kinshasa is a city of micro-infrastructures and the power of the minimum, where the exigency is to make as much as possible out of articulating imagination and small things, as well as insert oneself into every conceivable interstice, using whatever is available as a support for commercial activity. It is important to find just the right location to capture someone's fleeting inclination to buy something from you at a moment's notice, to perform everyday life as if it was full of abundance when in actuality most of the population is living with less than one US-Dollar a day.

As de Boeck (2012) indicates, Kinshasa is a city of the "now", in that it emphasizes the need for individuals to be prepared to act in many different places and in many different ways without warning, without preparation. This orientation reinforces the tentativeness of social life because the ability to affirm a collective body requires a sense of delay, of memory, and of rehearsing ways different backgrounds and capacities can work together. I talk to you, you talk to me, we talk to others, and in the process acquire memory and develop an understanding based on the delays involved in this process, the circuits of call and response and call again. But in Kinshasa the imperatives to act without reference, the immediacy of the all or nothing makes the consolidation of social life difficult.

Kinshasa is a city that both frightens and surprises itself with its endurance. So expressions of confidence take shape through these investments in the city's extension—to make habitable that which lies fallow. A bush is a city in waiting.

It does not seem to matter that these sentiments make daily life all the more difficult. Running around to manage an extended presence in the urban region leaves little time to tend to more localized relationships. In a city where many youth are deeply suspicious of the adults closest to them, where early death is usually explained as the malicious actions of immediate family, where the management of critical cultural conventions, usually the purview of elders, are seized upon by youth as expressions of the vacuum of any real authority, households would seem to make their current addresses more uninhabitable as the impulse for new habitation intensifies. So the relationship between the habitable and uninhabitable oscillates, diverges and reconnects in ways that make the provision of "new land" and new opportunities something that extends and builds upon the solidity of the existent city, but also seems to waste it at the same time.

In the ambiguity then of this relationship, we are reminded of what Michael Taussig (1980, 1984, 1995) talked about as devil pacts in his ethnographies of the Columbian Pacific. The determination to convert land into platforms for the production or extraction of things whose final use is elsewhere upends intricate ecological systems, which have provided living zones for creatures of all kinds. It generates wealth that can only be wasted. What is excessive to the necessity to live—the cultivation of cash crops, the effluvial toxicity of mined streams—and which takes the form of exorbitant profit can only be managed as a pact with the devil, as the willingness to undermine the very supports of life. The will to inhabit everything itself produces the uninhabitable through both the conceit that any part of the earth is available for habitation and the act of inhabiting which proves its own worth that needs no further justification. The immanent conclusion of this process is that there may be nowhere left to go, as these acts of inhabitation leave more extensive footprints—imprinted in every aspect of the earth and its atmosphere—undone only in unimaginable time scales (Morton 2013).

The extension of Kinshasa into its hinterlands prolongs a game that potentially runs out of space and time as the impacts of urbanization "talk back" through the shrinkage of virtuous terrain. As such, there is much worried discussion in Africa and Asia about the massive demographic shifts portended by climate change, about future impossibilities for the inhabitation of coastal and semi-arid cities. These are addressed through the acceleration of technological innovations that attempt to re-adapt populations to increasingly aquatic urban environments, that seek to mitigate the impacts of extreme weather or shift developments to what is considered safer ground. What I suggest is not so much that the designs and technicities of adaptation are not useful. Rather, we have to find ways of detaching them from the belief that they can prolong our normative orientations and will to habitation.

Equally troubling is the inversion of this position. Instead of acting as if all places and conditions are potentially habitable, incipient forms of urban governance act as if the ability to inhabit is not as important as the ability to 'ride the uninhabitable.' It is as if to "reside" means to "surf", to ride the crests, the ebbs and swells of greater or lesser turbulence (Braun 2014). To sustain a place is less important than to speed up the diffusion of crisis, to speed up the dissociation of places from cumbersome histories so that these places can be hedged against the other. Places become embodiments for the calculation of risks. They are emptied of specific content and repackaged as indices of investment, capable of turning damaged materials and lives into harvests of yet to be determined products or capacities. The emphasis here is on the ability to harness whatever takes place, whether habitable or not.

NO SECRETS ABOUT WHAT IS GOING ON

Even when coupled as the mirror image of our will to habitation, notions of the uninhabitable would seem anachronistic in light of the evidence it is possible to amass about the facts of where and how people live. If a certain part of the definition of the uninhabitable entails the extent to which a particular place is closed off from access to a larger world or is, in turn, relatively impermeable to incursions from the outside, then in this respect no place is uninhabitable. Even in the most seemingly depleted cities—Maiduguri, Bangui, Juba, Homs, or Gaza—there are doors to walk through. It is not the absence of doors, of ways in and out, that particular cities seem to lack, but rather a question of where these doors lead. Are they like doors in a large house, which lead progressively across spaces a person can feel as connected, as somehow linked to each other? Or do the doors open onto to some kind of "Alice in Wonderland" inverted reality, where the urgency of getting out of a particular city usually takes place only through doors that lead to completely disorienting experiences, and where it is nearly impossible to attain a foothold or a clear sense of what is going on? In a world where every inch of the earth's surface can be surveyed, from which information can be drawn and specific persons or buildings targeted, little remains unknown.

Once it was a matter of what surveying eyes were interested in paying attention to. Vast interiors of supposedly uninhabited neighborhoods were not worth the effort required to know or engage. For long periods of time, important population centers in major cities were not even designated on maps because they were bastions of illegal occupation and poverty. It was simply not worth paying attention to the *bidonvilles,* peri-urban settlements, shantytowns, or even long-honed popular working and lower middle class districts because there was nothing going on there of any importance. Nothing was taking place, and as such, there was nothing to see.

Such occlusion sometimes could operate to the advantage of a particular part of the city. In the outer regions of Khartoum's Omdurman district, where I lived for three years, just before the city met the desert, there was a densely compacted maze of mud structures that from the air appeared like the crumbling remains of some vast and abandoned way station. Yet, Souk Libya, as this place was known, was a pounding market where virtually everything was for sale, from the latest East Asian electronics to surface-to-air missiles to herds of sheep and camels. Brokers of at least fifteen different African nationalities controlled specific sectors of the market and traders came from as far as Nigeria, the Democratic Republic of Congo and Tanzania, mediating deals across the Middle East. Everyone in Khartoum claimed to have known about the market, had gone there once or twice, but it still acted as a public secret, a place beyond regulation and policing because at its surface it always exuded the sense that nothing happened there.

Now we live in an era where nothing is to be missed, where the prevailing assumption is that something is going on no matter how a place looks, and that all places are prospects for making money. The higher the risks, the more money there is to be potentially made or lost. Part of the impetus of this interest is the recognition that the purportedly abandoned or backward parts of the world are fertile grounds for the implantation of terrorists. Even if this may be the case, the capacity of such "invaders" to demonstrate the viability of these places as platforms for making money, may be more salient. The Sahara is a busy sea of transshipment of all kinds, and somehow the doors of the most seemingly marginal towns of Asia and Africa open directly onto Dubai and Guangzhou.

Of course within specific towns and cities there is great variance in the availability of particular doors, as many inhabitants are relegated to highly circumscribed spaces of operation; they may barely know anything outside their immediate vicinity, let alone anything about a larger world. No matter how much the world may come to them, through media, cellphones, internet, information and rumor, most of the doors available are to the same room. There are times when these doors are tightly controlled, as if in a larger world of operations it is important to keep too many prying eyes away in order to protect the little you have or to exert a semblance of control over a capacity to reach beyond it.

Just like Chungking Mansions in Hong Kong, that one square-block long warren of "guesthouses", small restaurants, and trading stalls, which has for long served as a favorite metaphor for the opacities of "old school" international trade, and is divided up into different turf, where exits, stairwells, and elevators are "secured" by various groups, much conflict in cities is also about "controlling the doors"—the entrances and exits. In Maiduguri, Nigeria, for example, the intensity of violence deployed by Boko Haram is largely about controlling where the doors will go. In its seemingly pathological fear of education and all public institutions, it senses that the extinction of the poor is through a door right around the corner and that the only thing they have to work with is an adamant and stark rendering of faith (Agbiboa 2013).

For many urban inhabitants walking through doors has left them feeling that their lives are situated in the middle of the doorway, that no matter how many thresholds they cross they are somewhere in the middle between the habitable and uninhabitable, no matter how much knowledge they may have about any given place in their city. This is an ambivalence that all the information saturated tagging of environments will not undo. No matter how available regression analyzed correlations among real estate values, availability of amenities, public services, history of property transactions, rates of growth, demographic profiles, capital investments, and local government budgetary allocations may be to any smart phone user inquiring about a specific location, a gnawing sense of uncertainty may remain (Fisher 2014, Stiegler 2013).

In Bangkok, for example, the city always tries to "retain face" throughout all efforts to deface it. In other words, the city remains full of markers—the surfaces of shrines, historical monuments, sexual economies, and mass consumption—that seemingly provide an unyielding sense of history and orientation. This prolonging of a sense of distinctive doors that interconnect different spaces of life into virtuous contiguities entails the responsibility to forget. The Bangkok resident must forget that the need to retain the calmness of surfaces, this sense that one door leads to other, from the king to monk to the shopkeeper to the businessmen to the sex worker to the tourist, has wrecked havoc on the city in terms of its infrastructure, natural resources and built environment (King 2008). Across many of the cheap condominiums where many Bangkok residents now live, there is an incessant anxiety with the appearance of ghosts, spurring discussions about the yearning for the happiness of an earlier time, however entangled with poverty and messiness it may have been (Johnson 2013). At the same time, there is an abiding fascination with all of the hyper-sexualized and disembodied digital landscapes that would seem to suggest the undoing of the cultural references through which that former happiness is expressed.

This ambivalence suggests a critical conundrum in working through the politics of habitation. For who is to determine what is habitable or not, and according to what criteria? How do we take the present distribution of habitation across many places normatively considered to be inhabitable and decide where people can live or not, and under what circumstances? In the exigencies to raise money for needed infrastructure, to provide work for a more youthful urban population, to work out more functional balances between maximizing the value of physical assets and assuring that the city remains affordable for its residents, the standards used in constituting normative habitation become more homogeneous and constrained precisely during an era where we are more aware then ever of the sheer plurality of situations that people are inhabiting.

In providing a narrower series of formats for how people live, and for spatializing the distribution of these formats in ways that require many to live at great distances from "where the action is" (without having much action really going on in the places they do live), the doors that residents navigate increasingly lead onto an open-ended, generalized world. The features of this world may be easily recognizable but without much of a sense of differentiation, anchorage, or mediation. No matter how race-infused the sensibility of *us and them* might have been, doors now seem to open up onto a diffuse sense of *us and us,* where inhabitants have to figure themselves out in relationship to a largely undifferentiated world of other individuals in almost exactly the same boat as they are. These are doors that would seem to leave little room for exchange, reciprocity and collaboration (Berardi 2009).

For in the spaces of inhabitation where things and bodies did *not* seem properly spaced out or organized, and are now largely resented by many for their messiness, dysfunction, and the amount of time and effort required to make things work and for people to get along, there was often a dynamic practice of social interchange. Different ways of doing things had to pass through each other, had to find ways to translate their differences, and sometimes made use of these differences as tools to assemble collaborations and deals between very different kinds of activities and backgrounds. Doors led to different experiences and spaces, and thus doors themselves meant something, either as rites of passage, infrastructures of mediation, tools for letting things in and out but in various exposures and intensities. Doors need not be open or closed all the way, but still allow different angles and perspectives (Bayat 2010, Millar 2014, Smart and Lin 2007, Telles and Hirata 2007, Vasudevan 2014).

How can we operate somewhere between the tightening standardization of habitation—with all pretenses to produce and regulate new types of individuals—and making the uninhabitable a "new norm", where value rests in what can be constantly converted, remade, or readapted? Such a middle is not so much a new "regime", imaginary, or place. Rather, it is a way of drawing lines of connection among the various instances and forms of habitation to find ways of making them have something to do with each other beyond the more abstract considerations of slums being reservoirs of cheap labor or that innovation always becomes fodder for gentrification.

WHY DOESN'T WHAT WORKS ACTUALLY WORK?

Today a key objective of urban transformation is to construct high-density affordable neighborhoods with sufficient green space, access to transportation and work, and which generate work through a diversity of residential and commercial composition. If this is indeed the case, then many of the so-called "popular", largely self-constructed districts mixing working and lower middle class inhabitants would seem to pose viable concretizations of this objective. For the past eight years, I have lived and worked in several intensely heterogeneous central city districts in Jakarta. These are districts replete with different residential histories, built environments, economic livelihoods, and social composition. During this time, I have had hundreds of opportunities for both formal and informal conversations with residents from very different walks of life.

Critically, these districts have never rested on their laurels, nor have they become calcified into a shaping of property that necessitates the defense of integrity or tradition. The capacity of such districts to accommodate, manage, and make the most of their heterogeneous composition is largely contingent upon continuous renovation and recalibration. It is hard work because if you want to create room for adaptation and for different economic activity and sociability to affect each other's productivity, then no single actor or activity should enjoy a disproportionate value or advantage.

Such districts may be at a disadvantage in terms of managing how energy, water, sanitation, waste removal, material inputs, and commodities are connected to each other in reliable fashion. But residents remain attuned to each other often through their very efforts to make, repair, and sustain the connections among these urban resources. Districts may not simply be crowded with people, but also crowded with aspirations, tactical maneuvers, and conflicts. These push their way out into district space and require significant expenditures of tolerance, local ingenuity, and mediation, as the strict delegation of responsibilities to specific individuals, groups or institutions cannot always come up with the adaptations necessary in a timely fashion. Because districts of such intensities may have to reproduce similar functions with a changing cast of characters, knowledge about how to run things is spread around. But at times it also leaves gaps in terms of deciding who has the authority to intervene in particular problems. In other words, advantages come with disadvantages; it is not an univocally clear story of win-win benefits. Nevertheless, there is much that can be worked with in terms of what already exists.

If you walk through the central city districts of Serdang, Utan Panjang, Sumar Batu, Cempeka Baru, and

Harapan Mulya in Central Jakarta, you will see an enormous diversity of residential situations. Like residents of any city, there may be many complaints and irritations. But these largely self-constructed areas provide both enough differences from each other to allow the congealing of particular lifestyles and affordances and enough commonality to mitigate any sense that residents of different walks of life constitute some kind of threat to each other.

The question becomes why such districts, embodying many of the characteristics that most urban policymakers and planners would want from so-called "sustainable development", are not viewed as the resources they indeed may be. While the majority of edifices may be small, rather cramped pavilions, there are no structural or prohibitive financial considerations that would prevent vertical development of four to five stories within the existent legal allowance. Could the infrastructure bear such a potential increase in population load? Here, again, Jakarta, through a past World Bank coordinated neighborhood improvement project demonstrated that significant increases in carrying capacity can take place *in situ* as long as conjunctions between primary and subsidiary systems are adjusted (Tunas and Peresthu 2010).

Undoubtedly, the location of such districts near the heart of the city exerts all kinds of pressures upon them, particularly as medium scale enterprises, such as banks, automobile dealerships, restaurant chains, and supermarkets extend outward, escalating land prices and drawing commercial-based revenues into municipal coffers. Still, many districts have demonstrated capabilities of rolling with these punches, as local entrepreneurial networks coalesce and up-scale their own operations or where residents themselves add on rooms to rent in order to cover increases in property taxes. The crux of these considerations seems to imply less the technical or fiscal impediments to the local productions of centrally located districts and more a very truncated image of exactly what exists across these districts and a limited view of just what can be viable.

This is not a matter of looking closer in order to discover a kernel of real truth and salvation. Keep in mind Joseph Conrad's injunction that the closer we look at things the less pretty they are. In fact, it is often hard to really tell what people are doing, why they are doing it, and where it all is going to take them.

When I step out of my house in Jakarta on a small lane and turn the corner into a busy street, I step into the midst of many things: I step into a seemingly interminable argument between two storekeepers over whose responsibility it is to make sure that the trash container does not overflow. I greet two young men who voluntarily sweep the streets for several hours every morning in order to strike up quick conversations with people waiting for transportation to go to work. I notice the beginning and endings of furtive couplings in the cheap by-the-hour hotels. I join the same convocation of customers at the small *warungs* (eating places), where we "compare notes" and plot both sensible and outrageous conspiracies to elevate our incomes. I sometimes join the lineup of devotees in front of the shabby office of a major local politician who moonlights as a spiritual advisor. I try to avoid the constant loading and unloading of trucks that in the frenzy frequently deliver goods to "wrong" destinations. I sometimes feel part of the constant milling about of people of all ages seeming to wait for real responsibilities but nevertheless feed the street with eyes and rumors. I am always surprised by the daily appearance of some new construction or alteration, of something going wrong and being left unfixed for only seconds or decades. I am in the midst of battered or bored lives going about pursuing the same routines and routes, as well as those who approach this street where they have spent every day of their lives as if it were the first time.

These multiple encounters and parallel, separated enactments, neither "good" nor "bad" are the substrate of the popular district. They are its real politics, even as hierarchies of authority and institutions are also obviously in place. Varying distributions of capacities—to affect and be affected, to bring things into relationship, to navigate actual or potential relations—are political matters. These are matters about who gets to acquire particular emotional patterns, thresholds, and triggers, and are connected to a complex virtual field of differential practice, what John Protevi (2009) calls *bodies politic*. What he means by body politic is the unfolding of a history of bodily experience, of *specific* modulations on ongoing processes of people and things encountering each other.

What we might think as the *virtual* is not some hidden potential that informs what a person's life could mean or the potentials lying in wait in any event. Rather, the virtual is the way that any encounter spins off into all kinds of directions and inclinations, as that encounter has enfolded different kinds of desires and perceptions to begin with. The question is where does this spinning off take someone, what will they make out of it, what other encounters will be sought out, avoided or accidentally impelled. This activation of the virtual—all of the encounters a person has inside and outside the house, at work, in the streets, in institutions—informs what a body is able to do at any particular time, where s/he does it, and what is possible to perceive and pay attention to in a given environment, as each body acts on, moves through other bodies.

This notion of *bodies politic* is important because it shows how the functioning of districts full of different kinds of people, backgrounds and activities does not work by residents forging some sense of community or that collaborations amongst them are primarily honed through a consensus of interests, division of labor, or proficient organizing techniques. Rather, things work out through an intensely politicized inter-mixing of different forces, capabilities, inclinations, styles, and opportunities that stretch and constrain what it is possible for residents of any given background or status to do. That no matter what formal structures, stories, powers, or institutions come to bear on what takes place, no matter how they leave their mark, that there is a constant process of encountering, pushing and pulling, wheeling and dealing, caring for and undermining. These encounters tend to keep most everyone "in play"—able to maneuver and pursue, if not all the time, at least for a portion of most days.

The persistent repetition, even hounding of urban residents, with the supposedly proper images of middle class attainment and overall well-being chip away at the convictions residents may retain about their abilities to construct viable living spaces for themselves. Time becomes an increasingly precious commodity, particularly as maximizing consumption and skill sets remain a critical indicator of self-worth. A younger generation of urban residents is more eager to escape the obligations of tending for parents and kin, let alone neighborhoods where the "rules" for belonging may become more stringent and politicized. A widening dispersal of interests and commitments are harder to piece together into complementary relationships and collaborations. The efforts at repairing and developing things that were once matters of voluntary association more and more seem to require a formalized, contractual deployment of labor.

There is a widespread sense that popular districts in Jakarta's urban core are finished, overladen with anachronistic business practices, excessive demands on people's time, and altogether too enmeshed in uncertainty to prove dynamic in the long run. Another consideration is the enduring frustration on the part of residents with the tedious bureaucracies, corruption, and wasted time entailed residing in the older formats of the urban core. At times there appears to be universal vilification of how bad things are run, and these images are not innocent as they are used to encourage resettlement in mega-complexes that exude the impression of efficiency and transparency, where everything is "run by the book."

But these impressions are tricky. Because neighborhoods increasingly vilified for being full of shakedowns, skewed deals, money lending, compounding interest, favors, sorcery, over-invoicing, re-sale, gambling, extortion, loaded gifts, kickbacks, pay-to-play, and hoarding then morph into statistical tendencies, branding, big data sets, probabilities, risk profiles, stochastic modeling, pre-emptive intervention, analytics-as-service, interoperable standards, clouds, and ubiquitous positioning whose ethical implications and efficacy are not necessarily more advanced or clearer. As thick social fabrics are torn asunder or coaxed into more individualistic pursuits of consumption and well-being, there are no clear visions or practices for how residents, still operating in close proximity to each other, will deal with each other in the long run, especially in circumstances where urban economies are unable to provide work for an increasingly youthful population.

Displacing outmoded urban governments with purportedly more efficient and transparent municipal administrations may provide momentary optimism to a more educated young generation of urban residents. But these municipal endeavors to ensure more than just environments for both the poor and middle class fail to grapple with the degree to which the real economic underpinnings of cities are largely configured elsewhere. A vast substrate of deals, accommodations, and compensations are necessary in order to sustain the lawfulness and efficacy of urban policy (Chatterjee 2011, Swyngedouw 2009).

Part of the issue is that many cities of the "South", no matter where they are, becomes subject to an increasing number of claims. The ability for anyone to definitively stake a claim necessitates widening interdependencies on relations and things that on the surface might not seem to have anything to do with a particular piece of land, building, or urban resource (Caldeira 2012, Gazdar and Mallah 2013, Goldman 2011, Raco et al. 2011, Ribera-Fumaz 2009). Dispossessions and repossessions then multiply (Banerjee-Guha 2010).

This proliferation of relationalities can be seen through the use of sophisticated number crunching packages, where a larger volume of relationships is made for us, instead of us trying to figure how things are connected. This figuring out of connections was one of the key skills and preoccupations of residents inhabiting popular districts. The figuring out in many ways was a practice of inhabitation. Now, parametric designs, which bring together different data sets related to water, finance, energy, transportation, housing, economy, individual and group behavior and so on, modulate the variable relationships among them, and alter their properties as a result. Water, energy and sanitation, financing, transport, municipal finance and economic development all impact on each other through recursive feedback loops (Parisi 2012).

While opening up new vistas of knowledge, new unpredictable and unfixable relationships are also produced in the very act of trying to better control things. In other words, we live in cities where things are *inevitably* linked and related, which gets rid of the will to actually make things relate — to coax, induce, seduce, incentivize. To move on then means to go nowhere, as one is locked into, indebted to being surrounded with all kinds of apparatuses—of recognition, security, legitimacy, correctness. Divisions are between those for whom interminable debts are required to stay in place—for not having the rug constantly pulled from under them—and those who are able to operate without any rug at all in almost any environment whatsoever. Here the uninhabitable becomes having a place in which to be located, whereas the habitable is the privilege of not needing any specific abode.

If the desire to figure out the relationships among things is diminished as a byproduct of increasingly formatted and programmed environments, then the very incentive for substantiating relational knowledge is undermined. This is the knowledge about how to act and make use of varying kinds of relations. However messy and untenable certain heterogeneous urban environments may have been, they were a context for the skilling of residents in the conduct of relations. These relations may not have been consistently generous, tolerant or wide-ranging. Nonetheless, they were "all over the place" and took inhabitants to many different "places" even if physically they covered little ground. There was a mixture of sentiments and practices that co-existed, uneasily, and sometimes destructively, but which nevertheless generated the capacities of residents to ply the potential resourcefulness of what they lived with (McFarlane 2011b, Moulaert and Nussbaumer 2005).

Part of the work of being in the city entails a range of literacies that have to be honed over time. Part of the importance of everyday urban practices is that they constitute a repository of urban learning, with important skills required in how to forge and conduct new relationships among people, places, and things. An important role for public policy then is how institutions can effectively pay attention to the logics and dynamics of the everyday in order to creatively animate a broader public awareness of the larger issues concerning the relationships between justice, redistribution, climate adaptation and infrastructural change.

Recasting urban life is then at the core of such a pedagogic, social learning project. If digital and new media are introducing new parameters for subjectivity, how do we think about new collective practices, focal and aggregation points so that new cultural practices can emerge? Rather than leaving the work of collective aggregation to consumption machines or so-called "fundamentalist" traditions, we need to explore new social contexts, procedures, modalities and institutions of social learning as ways of substantiating new ways of being together.

CONCLUSION

I want to conclude this essay with a concrete example of how residents in one district of Jakarta appear to navigate the interstices of the habitable and inhabitable that have been the "thicket" of consideration here. Kampung Rawa in central Jakarta, near the Senen rail station, was historically the port of call for many incoming migrants to the city. As the city's densest district, it is crammed to the hilt with a mix of long-term residents, mostly eking out a minimal income, and newcomers attracted to the possibilities for acquiring and remaking cheap property. The residents in this district have lived with strong ties to block-by-block solidarities, invented kinship relations among neighbors, as well as strong ties to tricks, scams, and petty parasitism in every sector of daily life. Its residents are widely known for maneuvering their way across different styles of being in the city, switching back and forth among performances of religious devotion, gangland bravado, entrepreneurial acumen, and inventive social and political collaborations.

Yet, the district remains heavily redlined by all official institutions; youth have a hard time getting more than low-level jobs. The place is so crowded that most household members have to take turns sleeping, leaving some to roam the streets at all hours. At the same time, more renovations and physical adaptations are going on in Kampung Rawa than in almost any other part of the city, and on any given day the place can be repeatedly celebrated and vilified by the same mouths. Whatever objective readings could be taken of the conditions here, the sense its residents make of the place seems to go in all kinds of directions. The words they use to identify themselves vary across a wide register, as does their assessments of the likely future. Is the place poor or not, safe or not, viable or not? Most residents can indeed provide detailed and reasonable answers either way. But the sense they make collectively remains something in-between, most are prepared to act strategically, no matter which way the answer goes.

It is important to keep this politics of sense making in mind as cities, particularly those in the so-called Global

South, are inundated with new imaginations, designs, and plans to make them more sustainable, just, productive, and generative of financial value. Regardless of the contradictions among these aspirations, a great deal of attention, money, and projects are brought to bear in cities like Kinshasa and Jakarta. As such, there is the need to more explicitly understand the political institutional gridlock that characterizes most cities. Whilst knowing the deleterious ecological footprint of urbanization, the systemic nature of the gridlock *and* the degrees and types of uncertainty involved, there is general consensus that a radical restructuration of the material base of cities will be absolutely necessity, even though few would seem to know how to bring this about or make substantial changes in their behaviour to do so.

Nevertheless, this necessity can be strategically engaged so as to produce new forms of sociality. This will entail piggybacking on and rewiring existing policy networks that cut across national divides, as well as forging interconnections among stylistically divergent local activist civic projects. But the intersection will less take place on abstract notions of cooperation or civic responsibility, but on the resonances among details—the specificities of how localities access and provision resources and opportunities, and how various kinds of articulation can be built among them.

While it is critical to continue to mobilize residents and municipal institutions to facilitate the endurance of residential and economic settings that have long provided affordable and effective contexts for the intersections of intensely heterogeneous backgrounds, built environments and ways of life, it is also important to find ways of re-describing the mass production of new residential settings where more and more residents are resituated.

Here, what appears to be the warehousing of the poor or the aspirant middle class in cheaply built high-rise tower blocks, may indeed mark the wearing away of long-honed relational skills and social economies. But they also may harbor the incipient formations of a process of translation, where certain details of past residential configurations are reworked in new forms. Many of my friends willingly have bought or rent small apartments in these complexes. I would ingenuously ask them, "How can you live in a place like this?" They often pointed out the possibilities of different forms of collective life, more provisional, perhaps ephemeral, but with a strong sense of possibility, and one not predicated on "going it alone", but of working out continuously mutable forms of interchange and interventions, with a commitment to use the apparently untenable as a means of rediscovering what it means to "go against the grain." If we only pay attention to the roll-out of contemporary spatial products as exemplars of urban neoliberalism, we might miss opportunities to see something else taking place, vulnerable and provisional though it may be.

REFERENCES

Adams, Ross Exo. "Natura Urbans, Natura Urbanata: Ecological urbanism, circulation, and the immunization of nature." *Environment and Planning D: Society and Space* 32 (2014): 12–29.

Agbiboa, Daniel E. "Boko Haram, Religious Violence and the Crisis of National Identity in Nigeria: Toward a Non-Killing Approach." *Journal of Developing Societies* 29, no. 4 (2013): 379–403.

Amin, Ash. "Surviving the Turbulent Future." *Environment and Planning D: Society and Space* 31 (2013): 140–156.

Amin, Samir. *Accumulation on a World Scale: A critique of the theory of underdevelopment*. New York; London: Monthly Review Press, 1974.

Banerjee-Guha, Swaptna (ed.). *Accumulation by Dispossession: Transformative Cities in the New Global Order*. Delhi: Sage, 2010.

Bayat, Asef. *Life as Politics: How Ordinary People Change the Middle East*. Stanford, CA: Stanford University Press, 2010.

Benjamin, Solomon. "Occupancy Urbanism: Radicalizing Politics and Economy Beyond Policy and Programs." *International Journal of Urban and Regional Research* 32, no. 3 (2008): 719–729.

Berardi, Franco "Bifo". *The Soul at Work: From Alienation to Autonomy*. Cambridge, MA: Semiotext(e)/MIT Press, 2009.

Bhalla, Ajit, and Frédéric Lapeyre. "Social Exclusion: Towards an Analytical and Operational Framework." *Development and Change* 28, no. 3 (1997): 413–433.

Blomley, Nicholas K. *Unsettling the City: Urban Land and the Politics of Property*. New York, NY: Routledge. 2004.

Boeck, Filip de. "Inhabiting ocular ground: Kinshasa's Future in the Light of Congo's Spectral Urban Politics." *Cultural Anthropology* 26, no. 2 (2011): 263–286.

___ "Spectral Kinshasa: Building the City through an Architecture of Words." In: *Urban Theory Beyond the West: A World of Cities*, edited by Tim Edensor and Mark Jayne, 311–328. London: Routledge, 2012.

Boeck, Filip de, and Marie-Françoise Plissart. *Kinshasa: tales of the invisible city*. Gent: Tervuren; Ludion: Royal Museum for Central Africa, 2004.

Braun, Bruce. "A New Urban Dispositif? Governing Life in the Age of Climate Change." *Environment and Planning D: Society and Space* 32 (2014): 49–64.

Brenner, Neil, and Christian Schmid. "Toward a New Epistemology of the Urban?" *City: analysis of urban trends, culture, theory, policy, action* 19, nos. 2–3 (2015): 151–182.

Caldeira, Teresa. P. R. "Imprinting and Moving Around: New Visibilities and Configurations of Public Space in São Paulo." *Public Culture* 24, no. 2 (2012): 385–441.

Chakrabarty, Dipesh. *Provincializing Europe. Postcolonial Thought and Historical Difference*. Princeton, NJ; London: Princeton University Press, 2000.

___"Postcolonial Studies and the Challenge of Climate Change." New Literary History 43, no. 1 (2012): 1–18.

Chatterjee, Ipsita. "Governance as 'Performed', Governance as 'Inscribed': New Urban Politics in Ahmedabad." *Urban Studies* 48, no. 12 (2011): 2571–2590.

Chattopadhyay, Swati. *Representing Calcutta: Modernity, Nationalism, and the Colonial Uncanny*. London; New York, NY: Taylor and Francis, 2006.

Chaudhury, Zahid R. "Subjects in Difference: Walter Benjamin, Frantz Fanon, and Postcolonial Theory." *Differences* 23, no. 1 (2012): 151–183.

Dawson, Ashley. "Surplus City." *Interventions: International Journal of Postcolonial Studies* 11, no. 1 (2009): 16–34.

Deleuze, Gilles. *Difference and Repetition*. New York, NY: Columbia University Press, 1995.

DiMuzio, Tim. "Governing Global Slums: The Biopolitics of Target 11." *Global Governance* 14, no. 3 (2008): 305–326.

Fisher, Mark. *Ghosts of My Life: Writings on Depression, Hauntology and Lost Future*. London: Zero Books, 2014.

Foucault, Michel. *Security, Territory, Population: Lectures at the Collège de France 1977–1978*. Translated by Graham Burchell. Basingstoke, Hants: Palgrave-MacMillan, 2009.

Fu, Albert, and Martin Murray. "Glorified Fantasies and Masterpieces of Deception on Importing Las Vegas into the 'New South Africa'." *International Journal of Urban and Regional Research* 38, no. 3 (2014): 843–863.

Gazdar, Haris, and Hussein Bux Mallah. "Informality and Political Violence in Karachi." *Urban Studies* 50, no. 15 (2013): 3099–3115

Ghertner, D. Asher. "Calculating Without Numbers: Aesthetic Governmentality in Delhi's Slums." *Economy and Society* 39, no. 2 (2010): 185–217.

Gidwani, Vinay and Rajyashree N. Reddy. "The Afterlives of 'Waste': Notes from India for a Minor History of Capitalist Surplus." Antipode 43, no. 5 (2011): 1625–1658.

Glassman, Jim. "Critical geography III: Critical development geography." *Progress in Human Geography* 35, no. 5 (2011): 705–711.

Glassman, Jim, and Abdi Ismail Samatar. "Development Geography and the Third-World State," *Progress in Human Geography* 21, no. 2 (1997): 164–198.

Goldman, Michael. "Speculative Urbanism and the Making of the Next World City." *International Journal of Urban and Regional Research* 35, no. 3 (2011): 555–581.

Hart, Gillian. "Geography and Development: Development/s Beyond Neoliberalism? Power, Culture, Political Economy." *Progress in Human Geography* 26, no. 6 (2002): 812–822.

Harvey, David. *The New Imperialism*. Oxford: Oxford University Press, 2003.

Heller, Peter, and Paul Evans. "Taking Tilly South: Durable Inequalities, Democratic Contestation, and Citizenship in the Southern Metropolis." *Theory and Society* 39 (2010): 433–450.

Heron, Nicholas. "The Ungovernable." *Angelaki Journal of the theoretical Humanities* 16, no. 2 (2011): 159–174.

Huyssen, Andreas (ed.). *Other Cities, Other Worlds: Urban Imaginaries in a Globalizing Age*. Durham, NC; London: Duke University Press, 2008.

Johnson, Andrew Alan. "Progress and its Ruins: Ghosts, Migrants, and the Uncanny in Thailand." *Cultural Anthropology* 28, no. 2 (2013): 299–319.

King, Anthony D. "Colonialism, urbanism and the capitalist world economy." *International Journal of Urban and Regional Research* 13, no. 1 (1989): 1–18.

King, Ross. "Bangkok Space, and Conditions of Possibility. *Environment and Planning D: Society and Space* 26, no. 2 (2008): 315–337.

Legg, Stephen. *Spaces of Colonialism: Delhi's Urban Governmentalities*. Oxford: Blackwell, 2007.

Lubeck, Paul, and John Walton. "Urban class conflict in Africa and Latin America: comparative analyses from a world systems perspective." *International Journal of Urban and Regional Research* 3, nos. 1–4 (1979): 3–28.

MacKinnon, Danny, and Kate Driscoll Derickson. "From Resilience to Resourcefulness: A Critique of Resilience Policy and Activism." *Progress in Human Geography* 37, no. 2 (2013): 253–270.

Marshall, Richard. *Emerging Urbanity: Global Urban Projects in the Asia Pacific Rim*. London; New York, NY: Routledge, 2003.

Mbembe, Achille. Critique de la raison nègre. Paris: La Découverte, 2013.

McCann, Eugene, and Kevin Ward. "Relationality/Territoriality: Toward a Conceptualization of Cities in the World." *Geoforum* 41 (2010): 175–184.

McFarlane Colin. *Learning the City: Knowledge and Translocal Assemblage*. Oxford: Wiley-Blackwell, 2011a.

___ "The City as a Machine for Learning." Transactions of the Institute of *British Geographers* 36, no. 3 (2011b): 360–376.

Millar, Kathleen. „The Precarious Present: Wageless Labor and Disrupted Life in Rio de Janeiro, Brazil." *Cultural Anthropology* 29, no. 1 (2014): 32–53.

Morton, Timothy. *Hyperobjects: Philosophy and Ecology after the End of the World*. Minneapolis, MN; London: University of Minnesota Press, 2013.

Moulaert, Frank, and Jacques Nussbaumer. "The Social Region Beyond the Territorial Dynamics of the Learning Economy." *The European Journal of Urban and Regional Studies* 12, no. 1 (2005): 45–64.

Napolitano, Valentina. "Anthropology and Traces." *Anthropological Theory* 15, no. 1 (2015): 47–67.

Negarestani, Reza. "The Labor of the Inhuman, Part II: The Inhuman." *e-flux* 53, no. 3 (2014), www.e-flux.com/issues/53-march-2014.

Nielsen, Morten. "Futures Within: Reversible Time and House-Building in Maputo, Mozambique." *Anthropological Theory* 11, no. 4 (2011): 397–423.

Parisi, Luciana. "Digital Design and Topological Control." *Theory, Culture and Society* 29 no. 4/5 (2012) 165–192.

Peck, Jamie, Nik Theodore, and Neil Brenner. "Neoliberal Urbanism: Models, Moments, Mutations." *SAIS Review* 29, no. 1 (2009): 49–66.

Protevi, John. *Political Affect: Connecting the Social and Somatic*. Minneapolis, MN; London: University of Minnesota Press, 2009.

Raco, Mike, Rob Imrie, and Wen-I Lin. "Community Governance, Critical Cosmopolitanism and Urban Change: Observations from Taipei, Taiwan." *International Journal of Urban and Regional Research* 35, no. 2 (2011): 274–294.

Ribera-Fumaz, Ramon. "From Urban Political Economy to Cultural Political Economy: Rethinking Culture and Economy in and beyond the Urban." *Progress in Human Geography* 33, no. 4 (2009): 447–465.

Robinson, Jennifer. "The Urban Now: Theorising Cities Beyond the New." *European Journal of Cultural Studies* 16, no. 6 (2013): 659–677.

Rossi, Ugo. "On Life as a Fictitious Commodity: Cities and the Bio-politics of Late Neoliberalism." *International Journal of Urban and Regional Research* 37, no. 3 (2013): 1067–1074.

Roy, Ananya. "The 21st Century Metropolis: New Geographies of Theory." *Regional Studies* 43, no. 6 (2009): 819–830.

Roy, Ananya, and Aihwa Ong (eds.). *Worlding Cities: Asian Experiments and the Art of Being Global*. Chichester: Wiley-Blackwell, 2011.

Sargeson, Sally. "Violence as Development: Land Expropriation and China's Urbanization." *The Journal of Peasant Studies* 40, no. 6 (2013): 1063–1085.

Shepherd, E., H. Leitner, and A. Maringanti. "Urban Pulse—Provincializing Global Urbanism: A Manifesto." *Urban Geography* 34, no. 7 (2013): 893–900.

Smart, Alan, and George C. S. Lin. "Local Capitalisms, Local Citizenship and Translocality: Rescaling from Below in the Pearl River Delta Region, China." *International Journal of Urban and Regional Research* 31, no. 2 (2007): 280–302.

Sparke, Matthew. "Everywhere But Always Somewhere: Critical Geographies of the Global South." *The Global South* 1, nos. 1–2 (2007): 117–126.

Stiegler Bernard. *What Makes Life Worth Living: A Pharmacology.* London: Polity Press, 2013.

Swyngedouw, Erik. „The Antinomies of the Postpolitical City: In Search of a Democratic Politics of Environmental Production." *International Journal of Urban and Regional Research* 33, no. 3 (2009): 601–620.

Taussig, Michael. *The Devil and Commodity Fetishism in South America.* Charlottesville, NC: University of North Carolina Press, 1980.

___ "Culture of Terror, Space of Death: Roger Casement's Putumayo Report and the Explanation of Torture." *Comparative Studies in Society and History* 26, no. 3 (1984): 467–497.

___ "The Sun Gives Without Receiving: An Old Story." *Comparative Studies in Society and History* 37, no. 2 (1995): 368–398.

Telles, Vera da Silva, and Daniel Velaso Hirata. "The City and Urban Practices: In the Uncertain Frontiers Between the Illegal, the Informal, and the Illicit." *Estudos Avançados* 21, no. 61 (2007): 173–191.

Thacker, Eugene. "The Shadows of Atheology: Epidemics, Power and Life after Foucault." *Theory, Culture and Society* 26, no. 6 (2009): 134–152.

Tunas, Devisari, and Andrea Peresthu. "The Self-Help Housing in Indonesia: The Only Option for the Poor?" *Habitat International* 34, no. 3 (2010): 315–322.

Vasudevan, A. "The Makeshift City Towards a Global Geography of Squatting." *Progress in Human Geography* 39, no. 3 (2014): 338–359.

Wright, Gwendolyn. "Building Global Modernisms." *Grey Room* 7 (2002): 124–134.

Zeiderman, Austin. "Living Dangerously: Biopolitics and Urban Citizenship in Bogatá, Columbia." *American Ethnologist* 40, no. 1 (2013): 71–87.

CARL SCHLETTWEIN LECTURES

The distinguished lecture of the Centre for African Studies Basel is held in remembrance of Dr h.c. Carl Schlettwein, who played an important part in the development of African Studies at Basel and in the establishment of our Centre. His moral support was supplemented by the generous and farsighted assistance he gave to these activities. Carl Schlettwein was born in Mecklenburg in 1925 and emigrated to South Africa in 1952. Until 1963 he lived in South West Africa, the former German colony that was then under South African administration. When he married Daniela Gsell he moved to Basel. In 1971 Schlettwein founded the Basler Afrika Bibliographien (BAB) as a library and publishing house in order to allow international institutions to access bibliographic information on South West Africa (Namibia). Accordingly, he published the first national bibliography on this African country. Through these activities the BAB contributed to documenting and researching a nation with a particularly difficult history. Other publications dealt with historical, literary and geo-methodological topics, and included titles on Swiss-African relations. From an individualistic private initiative, the BAB developed into an institution open to the public and became a cornerstone of the Centre for African Studies Basel. As the Namibia Resource

Centre—Southern Africa Library the institution is of world-wide importance. The Carl Schlettwein Stiftung, which was founded in 1994, runs the BAB and supports students and projects in Namibia as well as in other southern African countries. In 2001, the Carl Schlettwein Foundation funded the establishment of the Chair of African History, providing the basis for today's professorship in African History and the African Studies programme at the University of Basel. The Foundation works closely with the Centre for African Studies Basel to provide support for teaching and research and in 2016 it enabled the Centre to establish a position on Nambian and Southern African Studies. The University of Basel honoured Carl Schlettwein with an honorary doctorate in 1997.

Printed in the United States
By Bookmasters